# Where the High Winds Sing

A Naval Aviator's Poetry of War and Reflection

# Where the High Winds Sing

A Naval Aviator's Poetry of War and Reflection

by
Don Purdy

Illustrations & Photos
by the author unless otherwise noted

*Published by OK-3 Publishing,*
*26 Williams Dr., Annapolis, MD 21401*

ISBN 9798678032935

*Printed in the United States of America*

*Cover painting and design by Don Purdy*

For Eric and Kristine

&

In Memory
of

CDR Don "XO" Irwin
LCDR Roger "Red" Meyers
LCDR Dick "Batman" Perry
LCDR Dick Hartman
LCDR John Barr
LT Dave "Rock" Hodges
LT Mike "Mikey" Norwood
LTJG Fredric "Woody" Knapp
AMS3 R. M. Woynarski

*Until Valhalla!*

*"War is life multiplied by some number that no one has ever heard of."*

— Sebastian Junger

# Contents

# THE NUMBERS

As a Naval Aviator I flew the A-4 Skyhawk, a single-seat, single-engine attack jet, on 218 combat missions over North Vietnam from July 1967 through February 1969. I was a member of VA-164, the Ghostriders, one of the squadrons that comprised Carrier Air Wing Sixteen (CVW16) aboard USS Oriskany (CVA34) and Carrier Air Wing Twenty-One (CVW21) aboard USS Hancock (CVA19).

The loss rate for CVW16 was the highest of any Navy Air Wing during the Vietnam war and the highest for any Navy carrier since WWII. Eighteen pilots and aircrewmen were killed in action. Two enlisted sailors were lost in operational accidents on the ship. Seven pilots were prisoners of war. Twenty pilots and aircrewmen were rescued after bailing out of their stricken aircraft. CVW16 lost a total of thirty-nine aircraft. Fifty-five aircraft suffered battle damage. The Ghostriders lost seven pilots and one enlisted sailor.

VA-164 Ghostriders 1967
Official U.S. Navy Photograph

# PART 1: COMBAT

Painting *Off Target* by Don Purdy

## THE CALL OF THE HAWK

The hawk
seeks its prey
in the half-light of dawn

In the half-dark of dusk
the hawk returns
to the quiet of the mews

After dusk, before the dawn
when the last light is gone
the call of the hawk
echoes through time
over the Mekong
the Rhine
and the
Meuse

Flying combat missions and catapulting from and returning to land on the carrier became part of a demanding, daily routine. Yet now and then something— a piece of music, a passage in a book, a morning at sea, could break into that routine and remind one, for a few moments, that there was more to life than the war.

## THE LAUNCH

Whitecaps
stampede across a sun-sparkled sea

Shards of spray
shatter across the sky

The deck

rises

and

falls

on swells spawned
in distant squalls

Savor the open sea,
its excellent isolation

Escape the weight of war
a moment of contemplation

*Now, stand clear*
*of intakes and exhausts*
*Start all go aircraft*
*for the 0800 launch*

Acrid,
exhaust infused,
steam heated,
salt laden,
eye watering air
fills the open cockpit

> Close the canopy
> Start the engine

> Follow the signals
> of a yellow-shirted kid

> directing the jet
> with practiced ease

> across a chaotic
> oil slicked deck
> to the catapult

White-shirted shapes
scurry
from swirling clouds
of steam
with hands raised
thumbs up

> Catch the Shooter's*
> eye

> > Salute
> > Brace
> > Launch
> > Fight the G's
> > Focus
> > Breathe

> Fly

* Catapult Officer

# KNOCKIN' ON HELL'S DOOR

roll-in
eye on the target
  an arrow nocked
mindful of flak
and not
'cause I'm
  in the slot
  well taught
  mind locked
  one thought
  only got
  one shot

mid-dive
on the pickle
  a hammer cocked
pipper on target
altitude checked
ready to drop

four fifty knots
on the dot
  a screaming hawk
ejectors knock
eight bombs off
pull up roll right

flak's hot
glance back
  the wife of Lot
a salt block
taking stock
of what's been wrought

but

  we've hit this target before

they'll repair it tonight
we'll return at first light

  a rinse and repeat war

we'll come back later
to crater the crater

  'n you wonder what it's for

we'll roll the dice again
but you can't always win

  in a Bob Dylan score

because fate lays out the plot
and rewinds the clock

  knock knock knockin' on hell's door

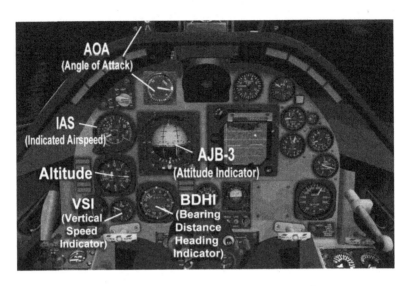

A-4E Skyhawk cockpit instrument panel

The night carrier landing is one of the most demanding challenges of naval aviation. Flying a small, cramped, unstable, single-seat, single-engine jet adds another layer of difficulty. Throw in rain and turbulence and you have a vertigo inducing mix that makes for some memorable, adrenaline fueled approaches. *Night Carrier Landing* is a stream of consciousness account of one such night and the constant battle to keep scanning and "believing the instruments" rather than the false sensations of vertigo.

## NIGHT CARRIER LANDING

"Marshal, Four One One at two one zero for forty-five. Angels one six. State two point two."
pitch black heading back in a monsoon squall taking

it in stages on the gauges put down the hook detach
from lead slow to holding speed

*"Four One One, weather six hundred overcast.
Visibility two miles.... Expected approach time two
eight"*

"Four One One.... Approach at two eight"
in and out of clouds talking out loud to my AJB3
attitude reference making a difference staying
glued to pitch and roll keeping an eye on VSI and
BDHI
"Four One One Established Angels one five. State
one point eight. "
'round the pattern turn and return....five minutes to
go....keeping an eye on VSI and BDHI now IAS and
Altitude check AJB3 attitude....two minutes to go....
damn vertigo feelings lie AJB3 VSI concentrate
fly....one minute to go.... AJB3 IAS VSI going high hell
of a ride stay inside take it in stages on the gauges

*"Ninety nine Marshal, Altimeter two niner eight
three. New final bearing zero one five."*

....thirty seconds to go....bend it around to
inbound....twenty seconds to go....watch the turn
scan and learn AJB3 IAS Altitude BDHI....fifteen
seconds to go.... Attitude Altitude IAS....ten seconds
to go....scan don't stare be aware vertigo messing
with me check AJB3 rolling out ready to shout...five
seconds to go.... four ...three....two....one

" Four One One commencing. State one point four."
throttle back penetrate right on time two fifty knots

on the dot coming down in the clag AJB3's reality ignore illusion wrong conclusion watch IAS BDHI VSI

*" Four One One, Switch approach. Button one six"*

"Approach, Four One One, State one point three." major madness damned darkness heavy rain AJB3 BDHI VSI bouncing around tightly wound just relax get the facts AJB3 BDHI Altitude IAS VSI cramped as it gets tiny jet BDHI VSI....Platform five thousand feet....power up slow the rate don't be late stay on speed AJB3 VSI IAS keep the spacing AJB3 VSI at the gate....twelve hundred feet....slow it up dirty up gear down flaps down check hook down all down no fear it's crazy Fly Navy middle of the night fuel's light BDHII, AJB3, Altitude, VSI, AOA now angle of attack's got my back stay on speed AOA all the way

*" Four One One, Approach, start your descent. Fifty low. Slightly right."*

" Four One One. "
no way to spend a night staring at instrument light vertigo induced universe reduced to cramped cockpit helmet squeezing stomach queezing head throbbing instruments bobbing bad thirst bladder 'bout to burst O2 mask oh too tight heart beating cold sweat beading AOA AJB3 VSI just fly

*" Four One One, you're on glidepath. On course. Four miles."*

goddamned canopy glare don't care info's there on the panel get a handle

*" Four One One, on glidepath. Slightly right.  Come
two left.  Three miles."*

scan the needles and numbers no blunders whoa
vertigo where we goin' stop slowing keep the speed
don't let it bleed AOA has the say wild ride look
outside nothing to see just the sea take it stages
back on the gauges

*"Four One One,  mile and a quarter.  Call the ball."*

driving rain turbulent air stay aware c'mon ship
where are you this won't do getting lower
windshield blower high concentrate fly ah is that a
light coming in sight whoa watch the altitude check
the attitude little right where's that light is that a
glow don't go low this ain't fair maybe there do I
dare give it a try trust my eye yes make the call
 " Four One One.  Scooter.  Ball.  One point one."

*"Roger ball. Deck's moving.  Right for line up."*

>meatball line up AOA
>concentration's salvation
>meatball line up AOA
>don't need no automation
>meatball line up AOA

*"Little high. Ease the power."*

>gonna catch me
>meatball line up AOA
>that number three
>meatball line up AOA
>no fear no fear

*"Don't chase it."*

    oh dear oh dear
    meatball line up AOA

*Little power. Power."*

    meatball line up AOA

*" Hold it. L i t t l e power. Little right."*

KABAAAM wheels slam full power VWOOOM hook
grabs jet slows eyeballs and hands got other plans
straps restrain stay in the game power back boards
in big grin jet stops roll back wire slack hook up
ease up wind down cheated death take a breath

*"Clear the landing area.  Clear my deck NOW."*

oops sorry Boss not over yet gotta move the jet ain't
no slack 'til in the pack shut down calm down play
it cool made it okay the Navy way ain't no casualty
open canopy casually plane captain running got the
ladder coming

*"Welcome back sir."*

"What?"
raining like heck forty knots over the deck too
much noise keep your poise getting wet not upset
won't show the sweat

*"Welcome back.  How's the bird? Hell of a night sir."*

"Howdy Joe. Bird's good to go. Yep a wild show."
hand him helmet and gear show no fear scramble

14

down dodge around intakes exhausts and props no
stops 'til island door thank the lord jump inside
escalator ride find the head beeline course pee like
a horse next stop maintenance shop yellow sheet
signed time to recline passageway ahead bathed in
red ready room none too soon collapse in a heap
standby for heat from the front row seats

*"'Bout time you got back, Jack."*
*"Anything left of the seat pan, Stan?"*
*"You look traumatized. Better see Doc for some*
*medicinal booze."*

"Nothing to it guys. Piece of cake if you're smooth."

## SONGS OF WAR

*Two-block Foxtrot*
*Turn into the wind*
*Man 'em up lads*
*We're goin' back again*

The squadron's sanguine song replays in my mind
as the strike group climbs away from the carrier

*We know what's in store*
*We've been there before*
*But that's the way it is*
*In this goddamn war*

We approach the coast where we'll turn south
for yet another strike on a battered
but unbroken bridge

*You know the way*
*Down to Thanh Hóa*
*To that damn bridge*
*'Cross the Sông Ma*

I move away
from my leader's wing
to that practical distance
where they can't kill
two birds with
one stone

The radio fills
with the taut litany
of combat

*"Red Crown, Tigers are feet dry,"*
*"Roger, Tiger. Bandits bull's-eye, heading 220, angels 12."*

and the sounds
of enemy radars
chorusing harsh tones
as they search
then lock on

*"Flak at twelve o'clock low;*
*85 two o'clock high!*
*Press on."*

Surface-to-Air Missile radars,
code name *Fan Song,*
trill alarms
in low tones
then high
as the SAMs seek
and find
their prey

*"Singer low! Watch it!*
*Singer high! Heads up, guys! Heads up!"*

A blood red light
in my line of sight
rhythmically mimes
the *Fan Song* song
in pulsing

adrenaline beats
*SAM   SAM   SAM*

I look;
raise my visor
strain to see
We all search
for the SAM,   then
the call we despise
but need to survive

*"SAM, ten o'clock low!"*

I don't see it
*"Heads up Tiger flight!"*
There! Coming so fast
*"It's on you! Tiger Four!"*
A contrail arrow
tipped with a missile
*"Break Tiger Four! Break left!"*
is tracking
tracking me
I turn
   it turns
I dive
   it dives

A red orange black white b l a s t
hits so hard
with heat so hot
I feel nothing

until

seared lungs
scream for air
in a sullied vacuum
of fire and smoke
and pieces;
pieces of missile
pieces of plane
pieces of me

Falling in a
spiraling pyre
I've got to get out! Eject!
But no arms reach
No hands fire
the ejection seat
to cast me out of hell
No hands key the mic
to call out, I'm hit!
to call for cover
to cry for help

I'm Tiger Four falling
    Falling
Is it that
    goddamn
dreadful
    dream
Falling
Wake me Annie.
Make those simple sacred sounds
in the kitchen as you open cupboards
and place pots and pans and cups and sing that song;

that song that wakes me from the dream once again.
*Monday Monday, so good to me...* Sing me out of illusion.
Drown out the saturnine psalm of roaring wind, the
wretched requiem with its disgusting promise
of eternal youth. Sing your song.

Seared, shrapnel-scarred
eyes cannot see
what's left of the plane
what's left of me

Blast deafened ears
cannot hear
the frantic calls

*"Tiger Four, eject! Eject! Get out!"*

Are they following me down
Are they looking for a chute
Are they wishing it was them
instead of me
Are they thanking God
it wasn't them

   So hot
thirsty
   spinning
in darkness
   loose straps
flailing
   battering
A torn, melted mask
clinging to my face

with stinging
starfish arms

I'm falling on fire
an unlucky
shooting star
shooting no more
A fated spot
on a radar plot
A well aimed shot's
foul reward

Everything hurts
I must be alive
It must be the dream

Falling
     Falling

The gravity I defied
defiling me

     Falling
twisting
     turning
tumbling
     drowning
grasping
     gasping

in the depths
     of the deep
dark sky

in a
spinning
   whirling
recurring
   recurring
dream

Wake me, Annie
   before I hit
the ground
   Please sing
your song
   soon

Are parts of me
falling with pieces of the jet?
Falling onto silver platter paddies,
onto the sun-silvered strands of a river, a beautiful
river, a beautiful *sông, một dòng sông đẹp.* Which *sông*
will take me in, salve my wounds in soothing
water; which *sông* will sing for me;
*Sông Ma? Sông Han? Sông Mê Kông?*
Which will restore me, wash me,
wake me, absolve me, save me?

Will they pick up
pieces of the jet and
craft the mangled metal ingeniously into useful things
like pots and pans and cups as they sing their patriotic
songs? Will pieces of me fatten the ducks; will they bury
the rest before vultures and crows cry
their cruel songs?

How long must I fall?
When will consciousness end and peace begin?
Where are you God? Have you forgotten me as I've
forgotten you? Forget me father for I have sinned?

Could you not send flights of angels to catch me as I fall?

Could you not
bind my wounds
quench my thirst
clothe me, feed me,
restore my sight
calm the storm
raise me from the dead

Or do you ignore the wounds of war in this devil's free-
for-all?

So cold now
and still
     falling
flailing
     twisting
tumbling

Annie, is that you? Ahh, at last, the cupboard door,
the pots and pans and cups, your beautiful voice
singing, *Monday Monday, so good to me...*

*"Tiger Four is down. No chute. Got the impact coordinates. KIA."*

*Two-block Foxtrot*
*Turn into the wind*
*Man 'em up lads*
*We're goin' back again*

# DUEL WITH A FLAK SITE

you sip tea
in a stilt house

I drink coffee
in a ready room

     as the sun washes night
     off the pink limbs of dawn

you walk a dirt levee
to an anti-aircraft gun

I walk a flight deck
to a bomb-laden jet

     as the sun polishes a highlight
     on the pewter mist

in my jet I come
high in the sky
a glint of light
silent until I dive
a silvery spec
growing in your sights
screaming now
but you cannot hear
over the pulsing
thunder of the gun
that stands between
you and oblivion

and sometime later
when the battle is done
you lie in a crater
twisted and torn
from the realm of time
but you did your duty

and I did mine

as the bloodied sun fell
before the night

# A Lesson from the School

It was a four-plane go,
a strike on a bridge at Tan Ky
with a replacement pilot
new to the combat show.

I'd been long at sea,
paid my dues; a hundred missions
going on two, but this guy had rank
so he had the lead.

Now as a general rule
this run is a breeze. But I told lead,
*"Avoid Nam Son 'cause we think
it's a gunnery school."*

We go feet dry
'n I'm 'bout to say, *"Don't go that way,"*
when BLAM BLAM, shots from Nam Son—
close, but a little high.

So we go on in
over the ridge, dodge some flak,
drop the bridge, 'n head on back—
the same way again!

Lead's in a hurry to go,
but too close to Nam Son. So my wingie 'n I,
(wantin' to stay alive), fall back and wait
for the fireworks show.

But then right off the bow
between lead 'n us, BLAM BLAM BLAM
on our height, just a little right
So I yell, *"Break left now!"*

27

I'm lookin' down,
Thinking *What the heck?*, when KABLAM!
Now that was close or... I've been hit
by an 85mm round.

If they tagged my ass
I'm gonna be mad 'cause where we were
means for sure, Nam Son U.
has an off campus class.

To see if I'd been shot,
my wingie joins up as we head for the coast.
He looks me over 'n says, "*Oh my gosh!*"
(an expression we used a lot).

My belly tank had a laceration
'bout two foot across, streamin' fuel, but not fire.
I'm still in the game, but a soldier used my plane
to get his shootin' certification.

Well, I made it back to the boat
'n got lead to agree, you gotta keep your cool.
Don't go by the school 'cause any fool can see,
it could'a been "all she wrote."

Aircraft 412 battle damage
Official U.S. Navy photograph

## THE MISSING MAN

Launch into the sultry haze
Gather the flight of four
Climb o'er a languid sea
toward the enemy shore

under a crystal canopy
swathed in sweat-soaked gear;
a hushed, helmeted sanctuary
safe from all but fear

'Til radar sweeps come alive
marking range, bearing, and height
with telltale gun and missile tones
heralding the coming fight

*"Switch to strike; Feet dry.*
*Master Arm on; combat spread.*
*Flak, level at twelve.*
*Tally the target, ten clicks ahead."*

Dodge and weave along the ridge
Charge through the dragon's gate
where tracers arc across the sky
red with rage, tinged with hate

Dark blots of flak burst
soiling the stark, sunlit scene,
random drops from fortune's pen
eclipsing my wingman's scream

His plane blossoms in scarlet flames
from the bud of an anti-aircraft round
then wilts in searing heat
and falls quietly toward the ground

*"Get out now! Eject! Eject!"*
But no answer to the plea
offers hope for a friend
mangled into a memory

No chute from out of the smoke
no voice from within the fire
no blessed white bloom of hope
from the silent, spiraling pyre

Return to Yankee Station
a somber flight of three;
a missing man formation,
a space where Two should be

Add his name to the chosen ones
appointed by the fates
Pack his gear and ship it home
to a widow in the States

Now from the vantage of age
appraise the faded scenes
Ponder the artist's intent
in a dark gallery of dreams

What war's cost was ever repaid
What war's lessons were ever learned
What memories ever replaced
those who never returned

Walk into the sultry haze
Gather at the Wall once more
Raise a hand to touch his name
far from the enemy shore

## COMBAT FLYER

you're a combat flyer
walkin' a tight wire
you always play it cool
    but fate loves a fool

you're better than other men
living on adrenaline
you're master of the sky
    but fate can also fly

you're the bandit's bane
you drive the women insane
and when you check your six
    you know fate's in the mix

you took on a triple-A gun
perhaps you could've won
but you made a second pass
    and fate got the last laugh

# THE LAST DAY

*for Roger "Red" Myers*

Red was flying patrol
honorably out of the fray

But he fought long and hard
to go in harm's way

When orders came to fly the A-4
Red joined us in the war

He accounted himself well
his courage never failed

He made the grade
His dues were paid

After seven months on the line
the last day arrived

Just one more launch
to make it through alive

On the catapult shot
his nose strut collapsed

The jet went into the sea
Red never got out

He went to war
He died a warrior

on the last damn flight
of the last damn day

## THE LAST FULL MEASURE

We launched day and night
from a seaborne lair
soaring to fight
in the war-torn air

Our courage a lever
in a political game
still we gave the last full measure
and filled a Wall with our brothers' names

# PART 2: AFTERMATH

Larry "Gruff" Duthie

Mike "Mule" Mullane

Jim "YDK" Waldron

Don "Inky" Purdy

Admiral Paul "Press On" Engel

After a burial service at Arlington National
Cemetery for a comrade whose remains had been
repatriated from Vietnam, I stopped by the Vietnam
Memorial, "The Wall." There were scattered rain
showers that day, but when the sun broke out, my
shadow on the Wall appeared to move as rivulets of
water cascaded down the polished black granite.

## A Shadow on the Wall

In sunlight it intrudes
spreading like a stain
It hides when darkness comes
It trembles in the rain

Defying my return
climbing up the Wall
it looms behind ranks
marked by fate to fall

It rises from charred remains
of valor's effigy
with the searing inquisition
Why them, not me

Side by side 'til they were gone
dare I ponder the cost
of death for them, but life for me
among the living, lost

Where a fragile calm belies the rage
spun by fate's wanton games,
the savage blasts that took their souls
and left only their names

Time once more to take my leave
to end the troublesome drill,
to watch the long shadow recede
then follow me up the hill

In sunlight it intrudes
spreading like a stain
It hides when darkness comes
It trembles in the rain

When the *Diagnostic and Statistical Manual of Mental Disorders IV* (DSM-IV) was published, survivor guilt was removed as a recognized specific diagnosis, and redefined as a significant symptom of post-traumatic stress disorder (PTSD). It is not an unusual response to surviving combat.

### LITANY FOR THE LOST

I dare not dwell
on that war in the air
on what I became
and had to bear
when I heard the names
but did not share
the fate of those who fell

I bid them farewell
in services at sea
that honored the souls
marked by decree
to grace the scrolls
writ randomly
by shot and shell

Now I repel
memories that loom
marching forward
returning too soon
when a flag is lowered
to a bugler's tune
I know too well

In a cloistered cell
of a personal war
my debt is due
in another encore
of that dark revue
that comes once more
at the Vespers bell

When solemn knells
rend the sky,
intonations
demanding replies,
lamentations
that multiply
in rising swells

I cannot quell
the mounting waves
that breach the shore
as my mind replays
the scenes I abhor
from the fateful days
I cannot dispel

When cruel cartels
of missiles and flak
demanded a fee
as we pressed the attack
with no guarantee
who would come back
from those trips to hell

And fortune as well
penned a scene
in tragic verse
that remained unseen
until we dispersed
and reconvened
at another farewell

Now who will tell
of the hidden cost
unknown to those
whose lives were lost,
who found repose
when they got off
this carousel

that spins a spell
and returns me there
to what I endure
but cannot share,
knowing for sure
it comes from where
I dare not dwell

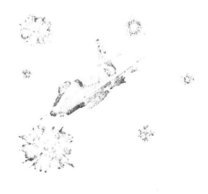

The U.S. Defense POW/MIA Accounting Agency has conducted joint field activities with the governments of Vietnam, Laos, and Cambodia to recover the remains of missing Americans. Since 1973, the remains of more than 1,000 Americans killed in the Vietnam War have been identified and returned to their families for burial with full military honors.

## REQUIEM REUNIONS

the war is over
but then
the call comes
as it has
again and again
since that
long ago fight
so we go
to Arlington
to reunite
to lay a brother to rest
again
at another memorial
that rends
old wounds open
again

we bury them
with honors
again and again
and unearth
the memories
when
the rifles fire
and the bugles play
at services
that never end at
amen

# An Unwritten Poem

letters
joined
in words
uncoined

speak of things
bound
in dressings yet
unwound

and sutures
unbroken
hold memories
unspoken

in a poem
hidden
deep in a wound
unwritten

### Full Military Honors

A flag draped coffin
  waits

The duty chaplain
  reads

A solemn choir sings
  an unanswered plea

>*"Lord, guard and guide the men who fly,*
>*Through the great spaces in the sky...*
>*Oh, hear us when we lift our prayer,*
>*For those in peril in the air!"*

Chapel doors
  unlatch
with a callous
  *clank*

An icy breeze
  barges in

A widow dressed in
  black
head held
  high
eyes willed
  dry
silently weeps
  within

as a somber scene
outside
  slowly
  sinks
  in

   A volley of orders, subdued and terse
   The Old Guard moving into place
   A riderless horse, boots reversed,
   nodding with stately grace

   A leathery, jingling clamor of tack
   A gravelly crunching of hooves
   The caisson creaking slowly back
   settling in grief-worn grooves

A requiem
of rolling drums
echoes

as a team of horses pulls

the coffin from
the 0900 service

remains repatriated
from the vicinity
of Hai Phong

a fallen husband, son,
father, friend

up a long
  cold
  road

          On the crest of a hill
          markers glisten with dew
          Aggrieved eyes fill
          An ancient rite begins anew

          The Lord is implored to receive
          a warrior lost in the sky
          Those blessed to believe
          must yet inquire, Why

A volley of shots
  *crack*
  the brittle air

A solitary bugle
  summons
  another
  soul
  to
  sleep

A tightly folded flag
   is presented:

*"On behalf of the
President of the United States,
the Chief of Naval Operations,
and a grateful nation..."*

A missing man formation
   *screams*
   overhead
   in a final
   salute

unheard by a widow
dressed in
   black
head held
   high
eyes willed
   dry
silently screaming
   within

as a somber scene
on a hill
   slowly
   sinks
   in

Friends breaking from ranks
solemnly gathering around
a coffin resting on planks
above a hole in the ground

A volley of orders, subdued and terse
A leathery, jingling clamor of tack
A riderless horse, boots reversed
accompanying the caisson back

to the Old Post Chapel
   where

a flag draped coffin
   waits

# THE DEBT

Is the debt of those we lost
the good they could have done
Does the task fall on us
who rolled the dice and won

Does fate demand a ransom
to settle up the score
Does fulfilling their dreams
end the endless war

If we shoulder their burden
the promise of their lives
what measures of success
ensure their hopes survive

Is a life well lived enough
Or do we owe them more
Does a fortune in guilt
pay the wages of war

## NO VACCINE

survivor
guilt
is war's
persistent parasite
that seeks out
those who live
and infects
their dreams
with thoughts
that accuse but never forgive
and whose
wounds
endure
for there
is no
c
u
r
e

## THE ARMY OF THE CHILDREN

A saber-sharp quill
scribes the bloody scrawl
absolving those who kill,
honoring those who fall

War's unholy water
fills the ancient fonts
consecrating the slaughter
*bénissant l'armée des enfants*

1915 Postcard

Vet Centers across the country provide a broad range of counseling, outreach, and referral services to combat Veterans and their families. Services for Veterans include individual and group counseling for PTSD.

## THE GROUP

They sit
> in a semi-circle
> facing an open door
>> eight defensible positions

They stare
> with old men's eyes
> at what young men saw
>> eight grim compositions

They say
> they're doing okay
> but as they sit and stare
>> eight faces betray
>> the one lie they share

# The New Guy

He sits down
in a circle of vets
He looks at their faces
and sees through
the "I'm OK" masks
Sees the firefights
that cloud their eyes
Hears the cries
that echo in their ears
Tastes the fear
that fouls their tongues
Smells the smoke
that flares their nostrils
Feels the pain
that pierces their souls

He leans over
forearms on knees
head down
fingers interlaced
as if to pray

*Dragging the body with as much care*
*as mortar rounds and ricochets allow,*
*he gathers his wits from the grip of fear,*
*and gasps for breath in the shell-shocked air*

*Huddled behind a wall, he says, Sarge, I'm okay*
*as he covers the body in a poncho,*
*grabs an ammo can, and runs screaming*
*back into the ancient city of Huế*

He flinches at the sound
when Doc asks,
Anything you want to say?

I'm okay,
he says,
But no,
not today

# HE'S A MATRYOSHKA DOLL

He's a matryoshka doll
of reinvented selves
struggling to hide
memories shelved
emotions inside

He's the solid one within
unbreakable marine
betrayed by his eyes
disfigured figurine
deep within the lies

*He was underneath*
*the bodies stacked on top*
*The one they found later*
*when the shelling stopped*
*down in the crater,*
*in the smoldering ground*
*under the other five*
*The last one they found*
*The only one alive*

He's a matryoshka doll
deep inside himself
unbreakable marine
can't unfeel what he's felt
can't unsee what he's seen

## HE SAYS

He says it was
covered in
bloody gauze

       Yet he can see
       that youthful face
       unblemished now


He says they were
lost in the din
of battle

       Yet he hears
       those last words
       clearly now


He says a chopper
lifted the lifeless
body away

       Yet he still feels
       the weight
       somehow


He says the time
and place
don't matter now

       Yet he cannot forget
       1968, Tết
       5 klicks northwest of Vũng Tàu

# PART 3: OTHER MEMORIES

Headed for a port call in Singapore, the ship was sailing on a clear night with bioluminescence in the wake and scattered about on the ocean surface. With a barely discernible horizon, it was easy to imagine that we were suspended between the stars in the sky and the "stars" of light on the ocean.

## MIDWATCH IN THE SOUTH CHINA SEA

A phosphorescent wake shimmering
toward the edge of night
meets the Milky Way
in a cosmic ring of light
as we ply a celestial sea
beyond the Pleiades
lost in the lyric
of a whispering breeze

The moment suspends the measure
of superficial notions
freeing captive spirits
to sail a timeless ocean
and chase the stars
across the night
until sea and sky
divide in the morning light

Another ship on another sea. *Lunar Interrogatories* references aspects of celestial navigation and the use of the marine sextant in obtaining a position from observations of the stars, the sun, and the moon. The perspective, however, is from the moon questioning the navigator.

## LUNAR INTERROGATORIES
### at 8° 31' North, 120° 53' East

What mystical tune
accompanied your tryst with the sixteenth rune
a cruel cabal so glaring and locally
apparent this noon?

And what brilliant stars
what famous flames with mysterious names,
Adara, Haedi, Izar, do you keep in books
like fireflies in jars?

Can we not conspire
in the evening hour to replay our refrain
in the chandelier light of a thousand stars
inflamed by desire?

Or are you lost within
angles and arcs, tables and charts
and mysterious lines that mark
the position you're in?

As the hour is aligned
for the measure of the mystical curve
of my lower limb, can we share time
with enchantment in mind?

And what will we see
in mirrored illusion, when you pull me down
with a gentle arm to kiss the salty lip
of the Sulu Sea?

After a moment entwined
on the horizon's line, will you turn away
as I embrace the predetermined arc
of my own decline?

Will my luminous face
now but a glowing trace of our embrace
be on your mind as you plot your lines
and close your sextant case?

Or must I take a final bow
as watch bells chime conveying the time
to follow twilight down and lift my crown
from the mountains of Mindanao?

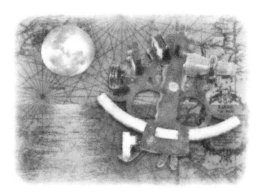

### MIDDLE ISLAND IDYLL

You waved from the shore
I stood at the rail
as the ship came into the bay

Cinnamon breezes
caressed satin sands
as champagne waves
whispered away
the tracks of time
and softly mimed
in rippled disguise
the selfsame moon
rhymed in your eyes

Starlight and desire
conspired to inspire
the night's delight
and enticed the day
to hold at bay
the sun's glow
as it lingered awhile
composing an ode
to your radiant smile

But time's demand
joined the ebbing tide
and bid my hand
draw to the side
a curtain of hair
on that face so fair
as couplets of tears
beckoned a sigh
that confirmed my fears

You waved from the shore
I stood at the rail
as the ship got underway

**LADY JESSIE**

Jessie Beck of Reno, Nevada was the first woman in the state to own a major casino. Dick Perry worked for Jessie while in college and they grew to be good friends.

When Dick became a Naval Aviator, he joined VA-164, one of the squadrons in Carrier Air Wing Sixteen aboard USS Oriskany.

Jessie kept in touch and started sending care packages. Jessie's giving continued as dozens, then hundreds, and eventually thousands of packages were sent to troops in Vietnam all across the US Armed Forces.

The Navy honored her by naming Dick's plane, and eventually all future Ghostrider CO's planes, LADY JESSIE.

LCDR Dick Perry was killed on a strike against the port of Hai Phong on August 31, 1967.
Jessie Beck died in 1987.

## WHERE THE HIGH WINDS SING
*for Lady Jessie*


Come dance with me where sunbeams stream
Through cumulus-columned halls of light
Share with me your secret scheme
East of the sun, west of the night

Come dance in carefree reverie
Through icy wisps of angels' wings
Embrace in airy ecstasy
Up where the high winds sing

Bank and roll and twirl in a dream
Climbing higher and higher
Upstage the grand celestial scene
Unbound by earthly desire

Dance my lively flying machine
'Til the starry evening is nigh
Then glide down a moonlit beam
Under a diamond-studded sky

Alight where kindred spirits are found
Let your flaming heart cool with a sigh
Endure the chains that tie you down
'Til once again we fly

*"I know them in a way I know no other men. I have never given anyone such trust. They were willing to guard something more precious than my life. They would have carried my reputation, the memory of me. It was part of the bargain we all made, the reason we were so willing to die for one another.*

*As long as I have memory, I will think of them all, every day. I am sure that when I leave this world, my last thought will be of my family and my comrades.....such good men."*

Michael Norman

Thank you to Larry Duthie, Mike Mullane, Jim Waldron, Larry Cunningham, Chuck Nelson, Sam Holmes, John Davis, and Bud Edney. You were the bravest comrades one could have hoped for when our lives were measured in moments. Through the years we have been lucky enough to share since then, you have been the truest of friends. To you and to all the Ghostriders who have passed on, my eternal gratitude.

Thank you to the men who worked tirelessly "behind the scenes" to keep the planes in the air and the squadron functioning in very difficult conditions. You never let up. You never failed us. You are the best of the best. Bravo Zulu!

# CODA

## Blood, Sweat, and Tears

Blood
The scarlet imprimatur
that sanctions the call
to arms

Sweat
The residue of fear
wrung from vestments
of war

Tears
The holy water that widows weep
to fill the ponds of martial mills
while war persists
to grind the grist
and grease the gears
with blood, sweat, and tears

'Leadership and comradeship'... David Williams-Ellis's sculpture in Ver-Sur-Mer, France

Don Purdy lives with his wife in Northern California where he spends time with other veterans at the local Vet Center and enjoys fly fishing, cycling, sailing, art, and writing when not attending to the needs of his master, Bogey.

OK-3
PUBLISHING
Annapolis, MD

Made in the USA
Coppell, TX
22 November 2020